Unique Learner Books

Unique Learner Books are learner books for younger people.

HOOPER DE WHOOP-WHOOPER THINKER LEARNS HIS NUMBERS!

By Doc Keagan

HICE PUBLISHING
Unique Learner Books

DocKeagan.com

Printed in the United States of America
Published by Playing With Plays LLC

ISBN: 9781954571150

For Rosie and Violet
May counting always be easy for you!

"I'm going to the train station!"
Hooper thinks.
That's curious, his pet tiger on the train
sort of looks like a lynx.

One monkey
in the
train car.

Two snakes in the train car.

Three apes
in the
train car.

Five hippopotami
in the
train car.

Six flamingos
in the
train car.

Seven giraffes in the train car.

Eight gibbons
in the
train car.

Nine bears
in the
train car.

Ten alligators
in the
train car.

But where's that one missing alligator?
Hooper said, "He'll miss the zoo!"
His pet tiger stood up on the beach.
Since the swamp was deeply blue.

Hooper looked and then he said,
"Perhaps we should leave? Later gator!"
Wait, here he comes now!
Full of splash and "WOW!"

Eleven cheetahs
in the
train car.

Twelve lions
in the
train car.

Thirteen tapirs
in the
train car.

Fourteen elephant
shrews in
the train car.

Fifteen panda
bears in the
train car.

Sixteen camels in the train car.

Seventeen panthers
in the
train car.

Eighteen orangutans in the train car.

Nineteen macaws in the train car.

Twenty zebras
in the
train car.

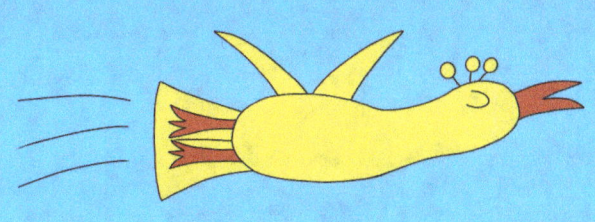

"I want to go to the zoo, too!"
said Rhiny the Rhinoceros.
Is Rhiny being a stinker?
Nope, he is being a Hooper De
Whoop-Whooper Thinker!

I want to go to the zoo, too!

Hooper was thinking that it was funny!
He was counting animals from 1 to 20!
Hooper got off at the train station!
Excited to see the zoo nation!

Hooper was a fantastic zoo counting boy!
Counting numbers filled him with
happiness and joy!
The zoo was fun and it's the end!
Hooper De Whoop-Whooper Thinker has
210 new friends!

And Hooper thought, "Good-Night!" and his pet tiger slept tight!

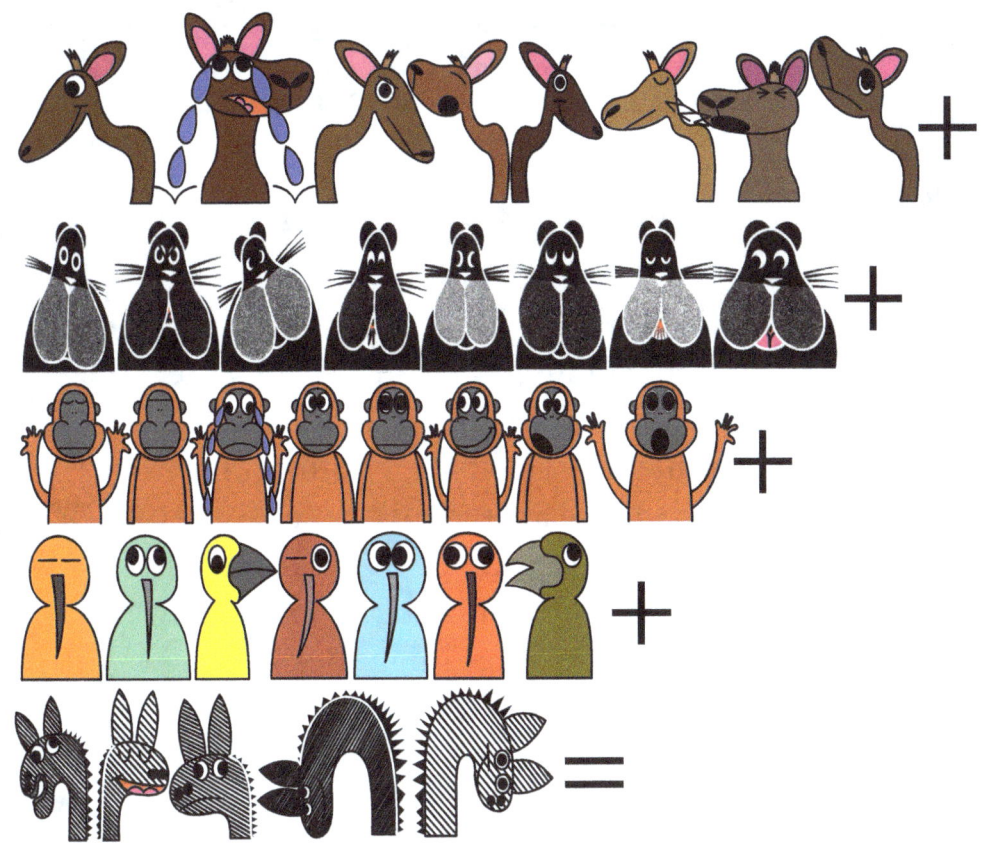

210

NEW FRIENDS!

Doc Keagan

Doc Keagan is an author and illustrator who writes both children's and adult books. He is inspired by the artwork of Dr. Seuss. His books, which are suitable for both younger and older readers, are reminiscent of Disney, Pixar, Muppets, Dreamworks, Nickelodeon, BlueSky, Columbia Pictures, Universal, Sony, Random House, They Might Be Giants, Barenaked Ladies, PBS, Paramount, and Peanuts. They are sure to bring back great memories for fans of Dr. Seuss. While he is new to the scene, Doc Keagan is already inspiring readers with his unique take on classic Dr. Seuss book titles.

Next published Unique Learner Book
coming up is Doc Keagan's ZYX!

www.ingramcontent.com/pod-product-compliance
Lightning Source LLC
Chambersburg PA
CBHW070944120626
46546CB00004B/1551